FUN STORIES

SEARCHING FOR MORE COWBELL

R. SCOTT MURPHY

R. Scott Murphy's Amazon Author Site and Book List
R. Scott Murphy on Apple Music and iTunes

SEARCHING FOR MORE COWBELL

Hello, Fun Stories Nation! Scott Murphy here. I'm so excited that you've come along to have some more fun. I have lots of new stories to share with you in an attempt to push random to new levels. As always, think of me as part storyteller, part game show host, part DJ, and part madcap tour guide.

Even as I write this, in some typical research facility with fancy glass walls, people in goggles and white lab coats are hard at work, trying to invent new medicines and other important things to make the world a better place. This is not that type of situation. Our goals here at *Fun Stories* are far less lofty. All we want is more smiles and laughs.

One of the most popular *Saturday Night Live* sketches of all-time is "More Cowbell." Aired on April 8, 2000, it spoofed the VH1 documentary series *Behind the Music*. The sketch supposedly took us behind the scenes of the recording session for the 1970s classic song "Don't Fear the Reaper" by Blue Oyster Cult. SNL host Christopher

Walken played the part of music producer "The" Bruce Dickinson, and Will Ferrell played fictional BOC member Gene Frenkle.

As the sketch unfolded, Ferrell aggressively played a cowbell, standing too close to the other band members as the group tried to record the song. His exuberant style irked the other musicians. Walken's character, however, seemed to enjoy it. He implored Ferrell to use "more cowbell." One of Walken's great bits of dialogue in the skit went like this: "Guess what? I've got a fever, and the only prescription is more cowbell!"

The phrase "more cowbell" became a staple in my life after watching that skit. The phrase can mean many different things to the people who enjoy it. For me, the phrase pushes one to have more fun, seek more adventure, and follow their dreams at a faster pace.

Because writing for *Fun Stories* is always so enjoyable for me, I often read through my rough drafts and tell myself that I need more cowbell. This encourages me to get closer to the finish line during the writing process. I hope that this edition of *Fun Stories* will help you better define your meaning of the words "more cowbell."

There's one other inspirational detail about the "More Cowbell" skit. Even though it almost always ranks at or near the top of any list of SNL's greatest sketches, Will Ferrell had to submit the script for the skit at least seven times before it finally made it on the show. Even then, the sketch was slotted near the end of the episode, where the more offbeat sketches are often aired. The lesson here is: Believe in yourself and dance to the beat of your own drum. The world will eventually dance along.

Here at *Fun Stories*, we celebrate random, odd, and offbeat stories. I sincerely thank you for taking the time to join our party. If you want to leave a comment, you can do so on the Fun Stories Facebook page, Twitter site, or on the website, mentalkickball.com. Again, thank you. You are greatly appreciated!

THE LEAST AMOUNT OF FAME POSSIBLE

(OLD MACDONALD RIDES AGAIN)

~

*Q*uick question for you, Fun Stories Nation. Past or present, what names come to mind when you hear the phrase "most famous people"? The names that enter my mind first are Elvis, Mick Jagger, Oprah, Muhammad Ali, Michael Jackson, Marilyn Monroe, George Washington, and countless other presidents. Debate it all you want, but these are all good candidates.

This is not that type of story. This story is about those less famous of us. It's about me achieving what I think is the least amount of fame possible. See if you agree with me after you've checked it out.

Once upon a time, I worked for the Texas Lottery. A large part of my job involved promotions. One of the biggest events in the state each year was the State Fair of Texas. It took place in Dallas and lasted more than three weeks.

As part of the promotions, I helped create an attraction on our sponsored area of the fairgrounds called the "Island of Fun." We sold lottery tickets, gave away prizes, and contracted with a national traveling game show for several daily performances.

Because I had quite a bit of TV and radio experience, I would get on stage and do promotions and updates on the microphone. Long story short, to get people warmed up for the game show, I started doing this bit on the microphone where I would say that I was Old MacDonald. You know, the one from the nursery rhyme who had a farm and a lot of animals. It made for great audience participation.

Full disclosure, my parents watched a lot of the TV show *Hee Haw* when I was a kid. It must have rubbed off on me. Wikipedia or YouTube that TV show if you don't know what I'm talking about.

Onstage at the State Fair of Texas, I'd recite the nursery rhyme into the microphone, get the crowd to respond with "E-I-E-I-O," and then pick people to come up on the stage, where they each had to act like a different animal and mimic the sound it makes. It was easy at first; people would be cows, pigs, horses, and the like. It was a lot of fun when we came to lesser-known animals such as linnets and magpies and people needed help from the crowd. This would go on for about 10 minutes and we'd end up with a good bunch of people. It was a fun, family-friendly game, and people enjoyed it.

I did this over the course of three State Fairs of Texas. Flash forward to more than a decade: I'm working a different job and I haven't even thought about Old MacDonald in years. I'm at Love Field in Dallas, waiting on a connecting flight. I'm pondering whether I'll get into trouble with my wife and my diet if I buy the large container of Milk Duds at the gift shop—you know, the important life questions.

I smile and say "Hello" to a lady in the gift shop who seems to be staring at me. Suddenly, she gets really excited. "I know you, I know you!" she says loudly enough for several people to start looking.

"Well, I used to work in radio and TV," I offer.

"No, no," she says. "That's not it." A light flashes in her eyes like a slot machine. "Oh my god! You're Old MacDonald!" she screams.

4

She jumps up and down like a contestant on "Family Feud" and yells for her husband to come over. He looks a little worried at first, but then his face too breaks into a smile. "Well, I'll be," he says. "It really is Old MacDonald!"

He enthusiastically tells me that I had chosen him to come up on stage at the State Fair of Texas and that he had oinked like a pig. He even won about $10 on some scratch tickets that I had awarded him. The couple came back the next year, and this time, his wife chose to be a horse in the Old MacDonald festivities, winning a t-shirt that she still had.

The lady fished her phone out of her purse and asked if I would take a picture with them. I said I'd be glad to, and she recruited another lady to snap it. The lady snapped 4–5 pictures as the husband and wife made intermittent animal noises. This instantly made the list of classic moments of my life!

Just then, a couple of other people in the airport quickly stood up and squeezed off camera phone pictures. I'm sure they had no idea what was going on but wanted a picture just in case they were witnessing someone really famous or something really popular. A lot of other people pointed at us and began discussing what was happening.

This experience was particularly funny to me because the excited woman and her husband had no idea what my name was. Sadly enough, I didn't get their names either. I shook hands with them and thanked them, and both of them hugged me like I was a blood relative visiting them for Thanksgiving dinner. It still makes me smile to think of how genuinely happy they both were to have met Old MacDonald.

While I am always grateful for anybody that recognizes me for doing almost anything, I feel like I reached a new level on that day. In my estimation, I successfully achieved the least amount of fame possible. And yet, it was quite nice.

I sincerely thank you, Airport Couple. You made my day. Heck, you made my whole month. If I ever get back in the farm animal game, I hope you'll agree to be my PR agents.

And I know you're wondering—yes, I did get myself the large container of Milk Duds. That's the way this Old MacDonald rolls!

SPECIAL NOTE: Make sure you see the Bonus Material section after the end of this book for more Old MacDonald information and a fun game!

NOT THE NEXT CARRIE UNDERWOOD

Now that we've established what might be the benchmark for the least amount of fame possible, it's time to tell the cautionary tale of what can happen when parents push young talent too hard, too quickly. "American Idol" has given talented folks like Carrie Underwood, Kelly Clarkson, Jennifer Hudson, and Chris Daughtry an opportunity to shine. For every one of these folks, however, there are millions of others that don't succeed. Sometimes, it's because they didn't get the right opportunity. And at other times, it's because their parents threw them into the deep end without a paddle. This is that type of story.

We'll call our subject "Shirley," simply because I love it when they say, "Stop calling me Shirley" in the classic comedy movie *Airplane.* Anyway, nine-year-old Shirley had shown promise well beyond the friendly confines of her elementary school talent shows. In fact, she regularly drew a room full of compliments after performances with the kids choir at our church. This is all next level stuff for a fourth grader.

To use sports terminology, Shirley soon got called up from the minor leagues to "The Show." This meant that the prodigy settled into a regular role with the adult choir. This was an unprecedented turn of events in our faith community. When Shirley made her debut with the adults, there were "She may be the next Carrie Underwood" whispers from several of the pews.

I didn't quite feel that Checotah type of magic happening in our neck of the woods, but Shirley seemed to be on a fast track. And, as you might imagine, the fast track would be her undoing.

Shirley's mom—straight out of Showbiz Mom 101—started Googling everything about Nashville. Let's call her "Moss." You know, the mother of the singer Shirley. As some of you know from reading some of my other stories, I love Google. Normally, Google is a very helpful tool. Too much Google, however, can sometimes have harmful effects.

Moss went into Google overdrive. Shirley had a new outfit for each Sunday session. Soon, Shirley's family invested in some expensive recording equipment that was professionally installed at the church. This also meant that Moss needed to hire an experienced studio person to record the Sunday services, especially the singing part. Shortly there-after, there were Shirley MP3s and Shirley ringtones on family phones. Moss even put up a website dedicated to Shirley's singing endeavors.

Then, Moss moved Heaven and Earth and did the impossible—She got Shirley the prime singing role in the Christmas Eve Candlelight Service, the soloist on "Silent Night." This is the crowning moment of the service, where the lights are dimmed and people pass the candle flame down the pews as "Silent Night" is performed. It's always quite a beautiful experience.

With a tip of the cap to the catchphrase of the "Lifestyles of the Rich and Famous" TV show host, Robin Leach, Moss believed the "Silent Night" solo to be the fast track to the champagne wishes and caviar dreams of the music world. This recording would surely make every decision maker in the music industry take notice of Shirley's talent!

A large banner was placed outside the church, announcing the Christmas Eve Candlelight Service. It also contained a sentence mentioning that the service would feature a solo by Shirley. Whoever heard of getting their singing prowess promoted on the church's Christmas Eve Candlelight Service banner? Moss surely bought that banner, but that was a baller move that even the Kardashians would respect!

The banner did its job of turning up the volume on the idea that Shirley was now a local celebrity. In fact, more than a few people asked Shirley to stand in front of the banner with them to take a picture. Soon, Shirley had an Instagram account and more than 1,000 followers. Rumor had it that Shirley had shown her friends her new professionally produced 8 x 10 promotional photos. They said her mom was negotiating with the local mall for an autograph signing session to raise money for charity. When did Moss find the time to sleep?

For the first time ever, the rehearsals for the Christmas Eve Candlelight Service were closed to the public. Heck, I didn't even know rehearsals for the Candlelight Service existed until a few people made sure I found out that I was not welcome to them. That Moss had really whet our appetites for some candlelight singing of "Silent Night!"

When Mack Brown coached football at the University of Texas, he asked fans to "Come early, stay late, be loud and wear orange." Change out the outfit to red and it was the same near-frenzied atmosphere for that year's Christmas Eve Candlelight Service. Our family arrived a full 60 minutes before the service to make sure we had good seats. Surprisingly, seating was already about 75% full by then. As they say, nothing draws a crowd like a crowd.

Moss repeatedly stepped up to the microphone to ensure that we knew that flash photography and cell phone recording were both strictly prohibited. She added that media people needed to identify themselves and receive the proper credentials. Once credentialed, they still were only allowed to record the first 30 seconds of "Silent

Night." I didn't see a single person wearing a media credential, but it made the whole event seem twice as cool.

Twenty minutes before the start of the service, Moss announced that the "performance" was at capacity and that a member of the fire department would not be allowing anybody else inside. Several folks still walked right in the door and squashed themselves into the small openings in some pews. I saw one guy in a blue shirt that might have known some firemen.

Finally, the service started. The air was ripe with excitement. Some people whispered that a group of suits near the recording equipment were record company talent scouts. A heretofore unknown group of musicians stood alongside the choir. There was a full drum set and a couple of guitarists. I hoped to see a cowbell, but I could not spot one.

People wondered aloud whether it was OK to give a standing ovation and cheer after the performance. The old-timers said there was the same feel in the air as when The Beatles had played on the Ed Sullivan Show. Again, the words "the next Carrie Underwood" were whispered around the room.

As we progressed through the service, everyone seemed to get tenser. Readers stumbled on words. The choir was a little out of sync. The pressure of the spotlight was getting to everyone. We had all allowed too much emphasis to be placed on one performance and lost focus on the reason for the season.

Finally, near the end of the service, the lights dimmed, the candles were distributed, and shiny faces glowed in the flame as it was passed down each row from person to person. The darkness and anticipation in the air gave it a feel similar to a Super Bowl halftime show.

The band performed tepidly, and the piano player hit each key too carefully because the recording equipment was at work. Shirley looked a little tense as she stepped up to the mic. Her usual smile was missing. This had officially become work for her. There was no joy in her eyes. Three different people, including her mom, were giving her hand signals. She stared at the recording engineer in the back and waited for his signal. He motioned for her to get a little closer to the microphone.

There was too much for her to worry about. Shirley was not having fun. She opened her mouth and began to sing. The first 30 seconds were a little uneven, but we knew our girl Shirley would push down the landing gear, bounce safely onto the runway, and pilot this flight to fame.

SOUND OF THE NEEDLE DRAGGING ACROSS A RECORD.

Well, at least that's what it sounded like to us. After wobbling into the ending of verse number one, our girl Shirley paused, stammered, and then completely blanked out on the words to verse two.

Horror filled her face and there were frantic hand signals from all over the room. We were confident that this was a temporary thing and the words would soon come back to her.

Unfortunately, that never happened. What did happen? I like to call it Shirley's "Frightmare Before Christmas." Shirley squirmed and looked around for help. None of the hand signals had a solution for the forgotten song lines. Shirley was not going to remember the words to the second verse—or any other verse—of "Silent Night." The entire song had abandoned her.

The piano player—seemingly on an audition of her own—showed no mercy. She dragged poor Shirley through verse after verse like a horse dragging a fallen rider behind it. Did you know "Silent Night" has six verses? Poor Shirley suffered, standing before the mic, through all of them.

She was reduced to humming and randomly saying "Jeeesuzz" and "Niiight" as the six verses dragged along at a snail's pace. At the start of each new verse, people clutched their fists in support or perhaps a desperate attempt to send positive vibes to Shirley. Then they would look down when nothing changed. Shirley simply didn't have it on this night. Finally, well after the sixth and last verse had started, someone tried to hand Shirley a hymnal to help with the words. But it was way too late for that to help her. Shirley just looked down and waited for the piano to stop.

When it was over, you could hear a pin drop. There were no claps, no holiday cheers—just teary eyes and parents hugging their kids tightly and praying this type of unfortunate event would never come knocking on their door. Poor Shirley just stood there, frozen in place. The first sound we heard was her mother's wails. Her dad picked Shirley up and carried her to the car. There would be no autographs, no encore, and no more talk about Nashville and talent scouts. In fact, Shirley's entire family would never set foot in our church again.

I almost took a picture of the banner outside as our family was leaving the church, but I decided I didn't need a picture to remember all of the sordid details. Poor Shirley. We all learned lots of valuable life lessons that night.

It's been a few years since this happened, but you can still hear about the Great Silent Night Debacle at church. I don't see Shirley very often around the neighborhood these days. Her parents enrolled her in a private school, and she looks very different from how she looked in fourth grade. I hear she's playing a lot of soccer now and is quite a good player.

Last week, they announced that a new soccer stadium was going to come up in Austin for a professional team that will call our area its new home. I sincerely hope this is an unrelated event and Moss is not involved.

RIDICULOUS MOVIE THEATER
RECIPES: BIGFOOT POPCORN

~

We'll start this next story by first agreeing that refreshments cost way too much at the movie theater but that it doesn't stop the majority of us from standing in slow-moving lines to hand over our hard-earned cash in exchange for popcorn, soda, candy, and many other things. This is the process I was painstakingly moving through the other day with my family. I had reached the point where I had my popcorn and was waiting at the condiment station for the man in front of me to finish using the machine that butters your popcorn. I generally love having control over the butter machine. Butter Machine Guy (BMG), however, was taking it to the extreme.

BMG kept bouncing the popcorn container up and down and then shoving it back under the butter machine spout to distribute the butter more evenly.

To properly paint the picture for you, he had purchased the ginormous upcoming blockbuster-movie keepsake bucket that doubles as a trash can and costs most people half of their month's salary. Speaking of painting, BMG was no Popcorn Picasso, but the container still looked pretty impressive in his hands.

I must say that I've been down this "let's distribute the butter evenly on our popcorn" road many times with the smaller popcorn tub. So, as a fellow butter-on-popcorn connoisseur, I tried to tell BMG that my oldest son had actually solved this problem about a year ago. You may already know this trick too. You acquire the large red straw that is usually intended for the Icee drinks. That red straw fits almost perfectly inside the spigot on the butter machine. This allows for the perfect distribution of butter, even to the deepest recesses of the popcorn bucket. This eliminates any need to toss up the popcorn as though you're making a pizza.

But as I started the story, BMG looked back at me, furrowed his brow, and gave me the stink eye like I was interrupting the most important event of his life so far. He was in no mood to chat with me, especially about his movie theater snack. Next, BMG made a grunting noise, reached out, and pulled the metal tin full of jalapenos completely out of its slot.

What the heck? I didn't know what to think. Is this a power move? Was I supposed to be impressed? BMG then began smashing the jalapenos down in the container with his left hand as he turned the metal tin sideways, which allowed him to pour out the jalapeno juice. He smashed them down harder and moved the tin around in circles so he could completely cover the butter-laden popcorn with the jalapeno juice.

Some people like to use the term "Bigfoot" when they see something they've never seen before. I've also heard the term used when people accidentally spot a celebrity. No matter which version of Bigfoot you prefer, this whole thing had officially become a Bigfoot experience for me. I kept staring at BMG's less-than-clean hands as they smashed the jalapenos to get the maximum amount of juice out of the tin.

I incorrectly surmised—and I surmise a lot, especially when I see Bigfoot in the movie theater—that he would then just put the jalapeno tin back into its slot without getting out any jalapenos. Instead, BMG completely put his other (right) hand into the metal tin and turned it into a highly useful scoop. He dutifully scooped out two heaping handfuls of jalapenos that he then dumped on top of the popcorn. It's good he bought the ginormous keepsake bucket. I couldn't quit staring; it was like watching a tennis match as my eyes bounced back and forth between the tongs that were meant for the removal of jalapenos and his large right hand scoop.

After another grunt, BMG set the jalapeno tin way over to the left —nowhere near the hole it normally lives in—and then quickly wiped both his hands on his jeans. Why? Because that's the way Bigfoot rolls. BMG stepped back a little and gave his makeshift jalapeno masterpiece a full-on stare down. He shook his head disapprovingly and deemed it not quite right. So, BMG placed his bucket on the counter and mashed the popcorn one final time—with both hands. It looked like he was about to go on a very long trip and trying to smash things into his suitcase before closing it. He then dutifully wiped his hands on his jeans for a second time, and he was gone.

The tennis match continued. Only now, I was staring back and forth between BMG walking away and the messy condiment station he had created with his Bigfoot brand of mayhem. There was butter and jalapeno juice everywhere. I was scared to look, but I knew that some of it was on the floor and that I was standing in it.

When BMG was about 10 feet away, he could sense my eyes following him. He flipped around and caught me staring at him like a pitcher picking a runner off first base. He actually growled like a horror movie villain and gave me another stink eye. Pardon the pun, but this was great theater.

I could go on for 10 more pages about all my Bigfoot-related thoughts. At that point, however, I decided to just walk across the lobby and use the other butter dispenser at the other condiment station. I had zero desire to use anything at my original condiment station. I also had to stop by the bathroom and wash my hands—for no particular reason.

What about you? Do you like jalapenos and/or jalapeno juice on your popcorn? Am I just freakin' crazy? Is BMG ahead of his time?

Final note, I was back at the same theater the other day, using the same condiment station where BMG had made his juicy jalapeno masterpiece. And guess what? The contents of the metal tin had changed. There were still jalapenos in the tin, but they were now packed in little plastic containers with lids. There was not a pair of tongs in sight.

Now, I wonder if other people are pulling the same gross jalapeno pouring trick as the stink-eyed man I had encountered. I also wonder what the people who buy nachos—the people who are really the ones using the jalapenos—think about the new plastic containers.

I also wonder—in the style of Mulder and Scully—if maybe this jalapeno situation is far bigger than I imagined. What if the nacho folks had also been "juicing" their movie snack before the big jalapeno change? And what about the pizza people? Is this why cheese is the best-selling slice? So that they can have their own jalapeno fun?

How likely is all of this? Is this a sinister plot to unnerve all of us as we seek a little solace from the real world and try to enjoy some over-priced movie snacks? I will continue to monitor the situation.

The truth is out there.

5

HOW NASA THINS THE HERD

∽

$\mathcal{I}$ was at the grocery store the other day and this woman in front of me in the checkout line had walked right out of the 1980s. And it wasn't the fun, *Stranger Things* version of the 1980s. She wore a "Kenny Rogers American Tour 1980" t-shirt and red parachute pants, and her hair was a very poor attempt to impersonate Farrah Fawcett.

Speaking of *Stranger Things*, she strangely seemed to enjoy frozen dinners. Her basket was inexplicably full of them. I fixated on all the different varieties of frozen dinners that slithered down the grocery store conveyor belt. I also wondered why there were no frozen pizzas in her cart.

For fun, I tried to match several of the frozen dinners with their appropriate Kenny Rogers song. I softly hummed "The Gambler," "Coward of the County," and "You Decorated My Life." I hadn't had so much interest in Kenny Rogers since the day I had found out he once dated my all-time favorite model from *The Price Is Right*, Dian Parkinson.

And then it happened.

The 80s lady dug through her huge purse, frowned, and asked for a pen so she could pay for her frozen things with a check. For me, watching people slowly write out checks at the grocery store is the equivalent of being tied up in a chair and being subjected to incessant fingernail scraping on a chalkboard. If I'm ever captured by a hostile foreign force, they wouldn't need weapons to subdue me. They just need to start slowly writing checks and follow that up by slowly updating their check register.

Even worse, she discovered, after endlessly pulling items out of her purse, that she had left her checkbook at home. I tried to maintain a safe distance from all the used Kleenex tissues she was depositing everywhere. A long line formed behind me as she ransacked her purse. Her voice quivered more and more as she declared with each item that it was not the checkbook. It was obviously not her day.

Just as I was reaching my happy place in my mind, she made eye contact with me and let out an uncomfortable sigh. This was the part where I was expected to offer her some kind of comfort phrase. I like to tell stories, but I had nothing for her that day. She had caught me at a selfish time. The pre-game for the World Series was coming on TV in less than 15 minutes; I had planned my entire day around the game.

I promise I'm better than this on most days. I did make a sad face for her and offer half a head bow, however. It probably scored very low on the comfort scale. Bottom line, I'm probably not the best candidate to write any of those "Chicken Soup for the Soul" stories.

My neighbors in line? They were far less accommodating than me. It began to rain snippy comments. The grocery store cashier began to feel the heat. Irritated, he asked the lady, "How can we resolve this?"

Checkbook Lady let out a long sniffle—I think it was mostly acting—and paused for dramatic effect. She then said, "My life is just so complicated right now that I need some of those smart people at Nassau to help me figure it out. Nassau would know what to do."

Oh my...

I briefly made eye contact with the checkout guy, but we both looked away quickly. Now, I had another dilemma. I had no idea if it was Nassau, Florida or Nassau in the Bahamas. I'm 99% certain, however, that Checkbook Lady needed a refresher course about America's space program.

To add an extra layer to this story, I had just toured NASA's Houston operation a few months earlier because my wife has relatives who work there. This was a lot to process while I was already worrying about the World Series and simultaneously beating myself up inside because I could not remember more Kenny Rogers songs. It really bugged me that the number of frozen dinners she was buying was greater than the number of Kenny Rogers songs I could remember. Casey Kasem would not be pleased.

Good news. Checkbook Lady found some cash in her purse and bought most of her groceries. She had to leave two frozen dinners behind. She headed for the exit, as those frozen dinners joined the array of items running through my mind.

Flashbacks ensued. My mom used to give me those Swanson Chicken frozen dinners when I was a kid. Random events trigger more random memories for me—most of the time.

More good news, I made it home for most of the pre-game show. Even so, I had to grab my phone and Google Up, because I'm the Freakin' Michael Phelps of Googling. Before the first pitch of the World Series baseball game, I watched the Port Nassau Webcam, read some part of the Bahamas Vacation Guide, and swiped through a slideshow of the Top 10 Must-See Attractions in Nassau.

Poor NASA.

With an opportunity to learn more about space and rocket science, I took Checkbook Lady's lead and directed the whole surfing session toward vacation destinations. Don't worry about NASA. In fact, the plot twist of this story applies to both Checkbook Lady and me. NASA is a top-level operation. It has no time for this type of nonsense. News flash! This is how NASA thins the herd.

It's not too late for you, though. How can you succeed where Checkbook Lady and I failed? Learn more about NASA and don't ever write another check.

Now, I'm off to Google more about frozen dinners—and Kenny

Rogers. I must never be flat-footed again if ever I need to remember a greater number of songs by a music artist I heard as a kid than the number of frozen food items the person in front of me is purchasing. That's my own top-level stuff. It's my private version of NASA, baby!

Speaking of "The Gambler," do you remember the episode of "Seinfeld" that had a story arc about the Kenny Rogers chicken restaurant? The bright neon light from the restaurant's sign was taking over Kramer's apartment. Yes, I had to Google it. It is from Season 8, Episode 8 and it's called "The Chicken Roaster." Alright, that's enough Kenny Rogers already.

FRAUDULENT TEXAS MESSAGES

In this crazy, 24-hour news cycle world, news sites are in a ridiculously competitive race to be the first ones to post breaking news stories on the Internet. Sometimes, they get accused of posting fake news. Sometimes, they just plain make mistakes. A recent mistake hit too close to home for me.

I saw a "Breaking News" message in an aggressive font as I was scrolling through the local news app during my morning wait for the shower. It was bold, in all caps, and practically screaming from the top of the news carrier's website. It claimed that we needed to "Beware of fraudulent texas messages."

Sure, I know autocorrect was hanging brain on the careless website headline writer, but doesn't anybody check these things anymore? It's mind boggling. Of course, it should have said "...fraudulent text messages."

It touched a nerve. Those of us that live in the Lone Star State pride ourselves in not ever sending fraudulent Texas messages.

I mean, it's just common decency, ya'll.

CRUNCHY ROADS, TAKE ME HOME

CRUNCHY ROADS, TAKE ME HOME

◇

Speaking of Texas, I have a fun winter driving story to share with you that includes the late-great singer John Denver. How's that for a random connection? Anyway, John Denver has a heartfelt song about West Virginia called "Take Me Home, Country Roads." You're probably playing the chorus in your mind right now. This is not a similar story. It is, however, a true story—about crunchy roads taking me home.

I attended undergraduate and graduate school at the University of Missouri in Columbia, Missouri. With apologies to Minnesota, North Dakota, Alaska, and such—the winters are sometimes pretty harsh in Columbia. Bottom line, after each cold winter, we would declare that it was shorts weather at Mizzou the minute the temperature reached 50 degrees.

I later moved to Austin, Texas, and had a very different experience with "cold" weather. The first time the temperature dropped to 50 degrees in Austin, people broke out their long johns and put on parkas. There were stocking caps and boots everywhere—and lots of fuzzy gloves. How could 50 degrees mean something so different to Texans?

Another comparison? While I was in college, they once closed one lane of I-70 after there was more than 20 inches of snowfall overnight in Columbia—and yeah, we still had class. There was not even any type of delay. In Austin, they closed my kids' schools a couple of years ago because there was a chance of ice. That's right, a *chance* of ice. Sure, better safe than sorry, but the temperature never got below freezing. There was a shortened school day, but there certainly was no ice.

Here's where the story gets crunchy. Full disclosure, it's been a number of years since I first moved to Austin. I'm sure road treatment has progressed at a rapid pace. On this December day, however, the sky looked threatening. I listened to the radio at work to hear updates. In a fashion similar to the chance-of-ice story above, they announced that schools and government offices were closing early because of a severe threat of ice. There was an 80% chance of it. The radio said we might want to stock up on water and groceries in case the ice paralyzed the city. Soon, our boss said we could go home early. This might just turn out to be the perfect storm.

Before leaving the office parking lot, I went over snow and ice driving tactics in my head. It had been about a year since I had driven on ice. I wanted to be on top of my driving game. I pulled onto I-35 and saw what I thought was a thin coat of ice. I gently tapped my brakes to test the conditions. I was being extra careful.

Upon further review, the road was making a "crunchy" noise. It sounded almost as if I was driving over a thin layer of potato chips. What was going on here? I suddenly realized I was driving on an insanely thick layer of salt—or whatever you called the road treatment mix at the time.

Scared of inclement weather, they had put down so much of the mix that it had formed a crunchy film on the road. It made for great comic relief. It also made me pretty hungry for barbecue potato chips

—my favorite potato chip flavor. I even considered driving on some side roads to see if any of them might be "extra crunchy."

The idea of crunchy roads triggered a song to start playing in my mind, which I hummed for the entire drive home.

"Almost Heaven—Austin, Texas." Fast forward to the chorus, "Take Me Home, Crunchy Roads…"

If anybody knows Adam Sandler or Weird Al, I would love to duet with them on that song! Now, I dare you to try and get the song out of your mind, which is guaranteed to be there for the next several hours. You're welcome!

8

GARAGE SALE GONZOS

~

*G*arage sales are like game shows on steroids. There is an "anything can happen, and it probably will today" type of atmosphere. You never know what you will find, who you will meet, or what will take place to lessen your enthusiasm for the human condition. For the past six years, we have held a Cougar Baseball Garage Sale for our local high school baseball team. It started when our oldest son played on the team and has carried on through the playing career of our youngest.

My wife started these events to help raise money for our program, and to try and differentiate us from the dozen or so other school programs that also try to raise money. It all seemed so innocent. Why wasn't any other team holding an annual garage sale? It's because, as I have discovered over the past six years, the overview of all this activity resembles the "Same Trailer, Different Park" title of Kacey Musgraves' Grammy-winning album. That analogy is especially fun for me because the baseball field is often called a "park" or "ballpark."

If you've ever walked around the grocery store and come across a wild-eyed person acting a little crazy, it is safe to assume that this person and all of their friends have probably been to all six of our Cougar Baseball Garage Sales. I call them "Gonzo Garage-Sale Goers." It's truly a team effort. We bring the items, and they bring the crazy.

Now, I'd like to share with you some of the lowlights of how we cut our teeth in the garage-sale game.

8 AM MEANS 6 AM

The first year, we set the garage-sale time for 8 am. This was on Craigslist, Facebook, LinkedIn, the school's electronic event flier, Friday night football game PA announcements, neighborhood association message boards, and our homemade signs. We had no idea that real garage-sale folks use that starting time as a mild suggestion. You see, if you are a GGSG, 8 am means the time when all of the best bargains are gone.

To further complicate matters, the Cougar Baseball Garage Sale takes place in early October; only about six weeks after the start of school. This means that we have pruned off all of the experienced senior parents from last year's booster club, and we sometimes don't even know the names of some of the new parents. Still, we expect them to pull their own weight and help with this event. That twisted logic is completely our fault, but this is volunteer work. We're all just trying to help the kids. Just don't try and rationalize all of this with the Gonzo Garage-Sale Goers.

So, half awake, my wife and I arrive at 6 am with lots of boxes. It is dark outside. There is very little street light. We're hoping by setting the arrival time at 6 am, most of our volunteers would arrive by 6:30 or 7:00 am. We are greeted by some faces we don't recognize. Just as I'm beginning to think we already have a great volunteer turnout and I'm trying to shake hands with some new booster clubbers, they start turning on their phone flashlights.

I suddenly feel like a zebra caught among a pack of lions. Several more phone flashlights go on. People start arguing about who was there first and what the order was for sorting through the boxes. One of them runs over to the concession stand because they have logically (and correctly) hypothesized that we had earlier stored many more boxes and several more tables of items inside it. Soon, several people are pressed up against the concession stand like it's the general admission line for Lollapalooza. I'm still not awake enough for my eyes to properly focus. I want to go home and never return, but we are doing this to help the kids. I repeat over and over out loud, "We are doing this to help the kids."

We place the first four boxes against the chain link fence away from the concession stand. Like a pack of wild animals, several gonzos tear into them and frantically wave their flashlights around as they check the sizes on some of the clothes.

It wasn't enough that they had ambushed us; now they wanted blood. "I thought there would be better items," one person whined. "I should have chosen one of the other sales. This is a disappointing start to my day," she added. Never mind we had a whole concession stand full of items and two more pickup trucks full of items on the way. I later found out that at that exact moment, one of the gonzos was already slamming us on the comments section of the Facebook event we had created.

We were glad to see a couple more friendly faces from the booster club arriving as we unlocked the concession stand. Gonzos wanted to follow us inside, but I finally snapped a little. I blocked them from the door by holding out the stool from a Guitar Hero drum set and putting a snarl in my voice. This was officially a circus. I told them to wait until we brought things out. I didn't even say "please," which is a rare occurrence for me.

As we carried out the first complete table of items, I kept my eye on one of the most valuable items we had to sell. One of the band parents had very generously donated an amplifier that had cost nearly $1,000 when new. It was just a couple of years old and in great condition. He felt like we might be able to get $200 for it in the garage-sale world.

One of the flashlights landed on it and a guy said it looked pristine. Hearing the word "pristine" made me cautiously optimistic that we were now getting up to speed with our fundraising efforts. "I'll give you $10 for it," he offered generously. I tried to politely tell him that it had cost nearly $1,000 a couple of years ago and was in great condition. I asked him to bear in mind that 100% of the money was going to help the Cougar Baseball Program. I explained that activities like baseball promote community involvement, plus they keep kids off the street and out of trouble.

Flashlight guy seemed to understand my words. "You're playing hardball with me," he said. "I'll give you $15, but that's my final offer and you have to carry it to my car." I wanted to tell him we were also selling fudge and that he should get fudge—a really funny phrase that my teenage friends and I used without getting into any trouble because the adults did not understand its real meaning. Instead, I used my best game-show voice to say, "You're wasting my time. No deal!"

He was not satisfied. He said, "Wasting your time? I thought you were a volunteer." This was so ridiculous that I picked up the amplifier and wordlessly carried it back into the concession stand. That's the garage-sale equivalent of taking your toys and going home. I'm not sure what happened to him because I sat on a purple Barney chair in the concession stand for the next five minutes. I needed to reset my attitude and take another shot at putting my best foot forward to help with the garage sale.

When I poked my head out again, even more gonzos had shown up to the sale. By 6:30 am—a full 90 minutes before the announced starting time—there were 17 gonzos and just five of us working the sale.

People complained that we were not selling refreshments at the concession stand. They complained that we didn't have enough electronics and said we shouldn't have included them in our ads. They said we needed more clothes for girls and a better selection of books. One person complained because there were no batteries in one of the remotes.

The game show "Let's Make A Deal" looks completely civilized compared to what went on all day at our sale. Gonzos love to bargain. I knew that would be the case, but I couldn't believe that people could look at me, knowing that I was trying to raise money for the school, and offer me $3 for an item priced at $20. Then, if I say $3 is too low, their counter-offer would be $3.25. This wasn't the trading floor on Wall Street. We were not dealing with Fortune 500 companies. We were trying to help kids play baseball.

One of the booster club members had gone around her neighborhood and collected around twenty pairs of jeans to sell. When I was haggling with one customer over 25 cents on an almost-new Ralph Lauren polo shirt, which was already a bargain at $5, someone stole four pairs of the jeans. They left the rest of them unfolded in a heap as they rummaged for their desired size. Who steals jeans from a high-school fundraiser? Even more puzzling, who steals anything from a garage sale? Karma surely evened the score with them at some point.

One lady from the booster club had made a couple dozen tacos for our workers. One person helped themselves to two free tacos and went home without buying anything. Another person agreed to buy a couple of toys, but only if they got two tacos and a bottled water from the concession stand. We bartered down to just one taco.

A DVD player had a $6 price on it. It even came with a free DVD; a reasonably successful Bruce Willis movie, I think. It seemed like a steal. People haggled to try and get the price down because the DVD player didn't have a remote and the DVD didn't have a case. I'm happy to report that I was able to get the full $6 for this item later in the day! Maybe the man from earlier was right and I was playing garage-sale hardball!

During a lull in the action later in the day, I was remarking to one of the new booster club members that garage-sale goers are unpredictable. Adding fuel to the fire, she told me that the previous year she had held a garage sale inside her own garage. About an hour before it ended, she had hid a present in the back of the garage. As soon as the sale ended, she was headed to her niece's birthday party. Right before the ending time, a group of ten people showed up, asking a bunch of questions. She called them gypsies. I hope that word is OK to use in today's world. Anyway, they asked a bunch of questions, lots of people talked at once, and then she later found that the present—and several other items—had been stolen. Again, who does this type of thing?

Allow me one more sidebar, please. Telling you about garage sale culture takes me to a completely different garage sale cultural experience I had a few years ago. My former neighbor worked for Dell and had gone on a two-year assignment to China. He rented his house to some folks from Taiwan.

I have to admit that I never really knew their names, but they always smiled and waved. We frequently shared quick conversations. They didn't speak a lot of English, but we talked about the weather. I enjoyed these interactions. I later progressed to being able to ask about their little girl.

After nearly two years went by, I received a Christmas card from our regular neighbor. It said he was coming back soon. Shortly thereafter, our doorbell rang. It was the lady next door. She had never rang the doorbell before. When I answered, she said in broken English, "Come to my garage sale." I smiled and asked her to tell me when she was having it and said I would definitely stop by. She motioned to follow her. "Now," she said. I felt safe enough, so I followed her.

There was no sign. There was nothing going on in the garage. The garage door was closed. Their cars were in the driveway. The yard was empty. We went right up to her front door and walked into her house. Her husband smiled and said, "Garage Sale!" over and over.

There were no tables and no items with price labels on them, but they were fashioning their own style of garage sale gonzo. "Make offer," the lady said and pointed at things like the TV, sofa, and the paintings on the wall. These nice folks wanted me to just point to things and offer them money. "Everything for sale," the man added.

I can't remember if I bought anything, but for several days after, strangers would pull up and ring their doorbell. The sale seemed to last for more than a week. I always wondered if they advertised the sale and if so, how they described it. I've also wondered if they sold everything. I saw the couch come out one day. Another day, I saw some beds being carried away.

Flash forward to the present. All good things, or mediocre things, or at least well-intentioned, back-breaking things must come to an end. My youngest son graduates this year. The booster club will be discontinuing the garage-sale fundraiser. Nobody wants to continue it once our family graduates from the program. It's not hardball. It's just a fact of life. We are proud, however, of some of the accomplishments we've celebrated because of the garage sales. Chiefly among those are the fact that we've raised a little more than $10,000 total over the years, and we don't think anybody has stolen anything for at least the past several years. That's a win in the volunteer world.

I continue to look around at advertisements for fundraisers at our school and at various other schools. I've never seen another local booster club have a garage sale. This does not mean we are unique. I think it's quite the contrary. I think these other booster clubs had older kids and more experience than us. In conclusion, they knew about gonzos before we us. Nonetheless, baseball season will be here soon. Go, Cougars!

9

BATHROOM WALL FAB FIVE

K nowledge comes from many different sources. Sometimes, you learn things from decorated authors such as William Shakespeare, Homer, or Charles Dickens. Sometimes, people like J.K. Rowling redefine our world. This is not one of those times. This is actually a quick story about what I recently learned from the bathroom wall of a major fast food restaurant chain.

I was traveling back to Austin from Dallas. I stopped at the fast food place in Waco for a beverage and a bathroom break. As the bathroom break was ending, I saw some graffiti on the wall. For whatever reason, I enjoy graffiti.

It's a mixed bag. Sometimes, you read things that are somewhat profound but most times, you just see phone numbers for girls and you wonder if they really exist. Sidebar, my wife's name is Jenny, and she actually loves that "867-5309/Jenny" song by Tommy Tutone.

This particular graffiti said, "Rank the Fab Five in order, then see my answers below." The only thing better than intriguing bathroom graffiti is two-part intriguing bathroom graffiti with an opportunity to rank things!

I tried to remember all the members of the "Fab Five" basketball team that played at the University of Michigan. I immediately thought of Chris Webber, Jalen Rose, and Juwan Howard. Then, the pieces easily fell into place because the other two are Texans. Ray Jackson is from Austin and Jimmy King is from Plano. Boom! Now, I had to put them in order.

Like those math problems where they give you the answer in the back of the textbook and you have to show your work, I looked for the answers to see how the Graffiti Guru had ranked the Fab Five. Would Juwan Howard's NBA longevity outweigh the raw talent of some of the others?

I found the answers just to the side of something that was definitely not Charmin. The answers were something completely different than what I was expecting to see.

Here's what it said:
5. Khloe
4. Kylie
3. Kourtney
2. Kim
1. Kendall

This had nothing to do with the Wolverines, or basketball, or the Fab Four of John, Paul, George, and Ringo that undoubtedly inspired the Fab Five nickname. Of course, at least 90% of you know that the graffiti Fab Five has nothing to do with being a McDonald's Basketball All-American. This Fab Five is a listing of the Kardashian women. As a dad, I hesitated to list the actual graffiti rankings of the Kardashian/Jenner daughters, but since they are all being included on a Fab Five team, I figured all the positions are all-stars.

I'm actually shocked that Kris Jenner, the mom, hasn't mined this Fab Five opportunity a long time ago. Like her or not, Kris Jenner is a freakin' marketing genius. I'm sure Harvard won't give her credit for her genius, but I'm completely sincere when I say that I think she is a genius. I'll bet no Ivy League professor earns anything close to what Kris Jenner makes each year, managing the vast empire she has built. I recently read somewhere that Kylie Jenner had become the youngest billionaire ever. Youngest. Billionaire. Ever. Kris Jenner, if you ever see this, please help me market these *Fun Stories* books!

Back to graffiti. Keep your eyes open when you're in the bathroom. Your next fun topic of conversation may be right there on the wall in front of you. If you see a good topic, share it with your fellow Mental Kickball players!

ALTERNATE ENDING:

This is how the story would have ended if I had written it when I was in college.

Keep your eyes open when you're in the bathroom. Your next fun topic of conversation may be right there on the wall in front of you. If you can't find the joke, it may be in your hand!

COLLEGE FLASHBACK:

Writing the Alternate Ending took me back to graffiti I once saw in the bathroom of a bar in Columbia, Missouri. Someone had written "Jesus Saves!" in black magic marker. At some later point, someone else added in red magic marker, "But Espo gets the rebound and scores!"

If you are completely lost, you're not alone. Phil Esposito was a hall of fame professional hockey player who scored lots of goals by rebounding the puck around the net and shooting it again. I'm watching out for bolts of lightning now because I shared the last part of this story.

OH, CRAP!

~

*I*t's getting harder and harder to get people's attention these days. People are addicted to social media, cranking loud music, battling on *Fortnite*, watching a movie on their tablet, binge-watching TV shows—and that's just my house. It's really difficult to break the clutter and communicate. Never fear, friends. I recently stumbled upon a pretty good solution.

If you need to make sure you have someone's attention when you need to say something, all you have to do is start the sentence with "Oh, crap!"

It's universal. When I say it at my house, my whole family looks at me—even the dog. I think it has a little bit of danger mixed into it. "Oh, crap!" just might mean everybody needs to stop, drop, and roll because I just accidentally started a fire. It might mean our Internet has gone down or we've run out of Doritos. Doesn't matter; it works every time. I'm wondering how many times I can use it before it makes me the boy who cried wolf!

"Oh, crap!" perks up people's ears, reels them in, and locks their attention on your words. Then, you give them an important message: "Don't forget it's trash night. So make sure all of that gets on the curb."

Have similar challenges at home? Try it today. Sure, I realize you could say, "Your attention, please," but isn't "Oh, crap!" a lot more fun?

ORGAN DONOR

I love Major League Baseball, but I didn't realize the folks at MLB knew how much. I recently ordered some online tickets for a Houston Astros game. During the process, they asked me if they could e-mail me about discounts, promotions, and special offers. Full of "the Astros might win the World Series again" glee, I checked the "yes" box.

A couple days later, I received an e-mail with the subject line "Special offer from the Astros." I expected some huge merchandise or ticket discount offer. I was actually kind of excited to open the e-mail. It was not what I was expecting.

It was not a discount offer or the announcement of an upcoming bobble head night. When I opened the e-mail, it said the Astros hoped I would become an organ donor. Yes, it is noble and good to be an organ donor, but did they have to ask me this in the very first e-mail? Please wine and dine me a little before you ask me for my organs, Astros!

Major League Baseball has all these theme nights now. There's Star Wars Night, Game of Thrones Night, Grateful Dead Night, etc.

This e-mail leads me to believe that we are not too far from having a Hannibal Lector Night. In fact, I'm really surprised that none of the Major League Baseball relief pitchers uses the theme music from "The Silence of the Lambs" as warmup music. That would be really cool.

Despite spending way too much time surfing on the subject, I could not find any minor league baseball team named "Lambs." Just when all hope seemed lost, I came across an exciting article. It said the Helena Brewers were relocating to Colorado Springs. It was announced that the team would be re-named through a name-the-team contest. One of the five finalists was the Colorado Springs Lamb Chops. This was a nod to what they claim is the largest and highest quality lamb in the world—the world famous Colorado Lamb. I was not aware that Colorado was so famous for its lambs.

Just as I was about to contact everybody I knew to try and get the team named the Lamb Chops, I noticed I was too late. Upon further clicking, I found that the team had been named the Rocky Mountain Vibes. This wasn't even one of the five finalists. What happened to bringing more attention to those world famous Colorado lambs?

As a consolation prize, however, I rediscovered some current and former MLB players with the last name "Lamb." Jake Lamb, a current player for Arizona, made the all-star team last year. I wonder if the Diamondbacks ever use him as part of their organ donation efforts.

JOE AND JILL SIX-PACK

e're going to talk about college and six-packs in this story, but it's not what you might expect. There will be no kegs and no beer pong.

My good buddy, Rob Last Name Withheld and I were college roommates at Mizzou. We mentioned it earlier in this book. That's the University of Missouri-Columbia, home of Truman the Tiger, with a pretty decent School of Journalism. I was in that J School and Rob was studying Education & Counseling Psychology when we lived together.

Even though our majors were vastly different, we always found ways to help each other. I worked as a reporter at the TV station and frequently needed what they called a "person on the street opinion." That's where you do a news story about a specific topic and get people's general opinions on the topic.

You try to get people who have an opinion on both sides of the issue. One of the professors at Mizzou called these people "Joe and Jill Six-Pack." It's a fun way of describing normal, everyday people. These stories happened almost every day. I needed dozens upon dozens of Joe and Jill Six-Packs to complete my stories. Most times, I played by the rules and found real people with real opinions. Sometimes, however, I had a hard time finding people willing to talk on camera. Yet other times, I was simply lazy. Walter Cronkite and the entire news world breathed a sigh of relief when I left hard news and went into advertising in grad school.

When I needed a "go to guy," to complete my TV story for those second and third kind of times, Rob was my man. It's especially fun because these Joe and Jill Six-Packs always get a serious graphic under their name from the news producer. One day, Rob appeared on the news with the graphic "Concerned Opera Fan" under his talking-head video.

Another day, he was "Citizen For More Taxes." I can't remember the exact verbiage, but there was also something about dog owners and public poop bags. It's pure John Mellencamp, "Ain't that America…little pink houses" type of stuff.

I'm pretty sure Rob could have won at least a People's Choice Award if he had gone into acting. Put some dollars and a major studio behind him and Rob could have won a pile of acting trophies.

On my part, I would help Rob by taking these standard psychology tests he was required to give as part of the requirements for some of his classes. Picture me walking into the Psychology Department lab with my St. Louis Cardinals baseball cap on backwards, wearing my Pink Floyd "Dark Side of the Moon" t-shirt. Rob was the go-to guy for TV stories. I was the go-to guy for psych tests.

We would look at ink blots, play word associations, and stuff like that. I felt like I was helping make the world a little better place by offering my input. Apparently, the choices on all these psychology tests could classify a person pretty quickly into a defined personality type.

Not me, however.

Rob would do a test, squint, and review the results again and again. He said he could never categorize me into any of the groups with these tests. That is usually a bad thing. My brain is evidently a mutant. He never said I was a potential serial killer, but my mind added that to the equation anyway. It was funny at the time. College humor is its own case study.

Bottom line, Rob made me promise to never do these types of psychological tests with anybody else. He was truly afraid of what might happen.

I've always heard that there is a fine line between insanity and creativity. Me? I'm clearly straddling that line and holding on for dear life.

REACHING THE END OF THE INTERNET

~

*H*aving a big imagination is almost as important as having a big, say it with me... heart. What? You thought I was going to say something else? You said something else, didn't you? Sure, that's pretty important as well. OK, it's official. I've managed to reach my target audience. You're my kind of people!

Basically, I like a lot of things in life, but when you ramp it up to love—well, that's another story. Without bringing religion or fast food into the conversation, I love: my family, my dog, baseball, all the crap I've put on my DVR, anything by Pink Floyd, lots of ice, car snacks, and I love my imagination.

Anything is possible if you have a healthy imagination. To me, it's far more important to work out your imagination than it is to work out your body. That is, unless Gold's Gym wants to sponsor these things. Then, I'll change my entire tune. I'll put a team together and work night and day to push apps onto your phone that sync with your GPS and lead you to any Gold's Gym within a hundred miles of your vehicle. I can try to do this for any company. Call me.

Yes, I love my imagination. God bless him, Robin Williams said we have the right to bear arms and the right to arm bears—whatever the hell we want. That's the type of fuel that helps my imagination run wild.

If you don't think creativity and imagination are a big deal, consider that I once worked with a guy who told me he had seen everything on the Internet.

I know, I'm really sorry—I'll give you a bigger warning the next time I tell you something so ridiculous and mind boggling.

BREATHE DEEPLY, EXHALE—PHEW.

OK, now that your mind has come back to room temperature, ponder that for a second. I'll come again—dude says he has seen everything on the Internet—and he honestly believed it.

Full disclosure, I was trying to save a few bucks and asked him who his Internet provider was and what it cost per month. I may have even used the "B" word—bundling. Everybody wants you to bundle things these days.

Who knew I could save money by purchasing cell phone service and toilet paper—all at the same time? This is why we're still the greatest country on Earth. I'm pretty sure it's interstellar domination, too. I'll bet they aren't bundling paper products and cell phone service on Mars or Jupiter.

So, getting back—dude says, "Uh, we don't do that anymore."

I say, "What—shop around for deals?"

He says, "No, the Internet."

He was so serious that I had to say the silliest thing I could think of at the time, "Wi-fi? Would you do that?"

He says, "First off, we don't do Netflix. So, after we saw some naked stuff, got a few recipes, and watched some moderately amusing pet videos, it all started to look the same."

He then said, "I think I saw everything there was to see on the Internet. I reached the end of it."

Dumbfounded, I just stood there like I'd been hit by Mr. Freeze's ray gun. It was worse than that time I mixed up "Wear your pajamas to school" day in fifth grade. Some of my oldest friends still call me "Scooby Doo Pants."

His words were so crazy that they kept echoing in my head, "I saw everything on the Internet. I saw everything. I reached the end." My mind created a mashup of it, but I couldn't contribute anything else to the conversation at this point.

I'm really sad that I missed a great opportunity. That guy lives for conspiracy theories. It was the perfect opening for me to tell him that the government could still track him because he used the Internet.

But no, I was a punch-drunk boxer taking a standing eight count. When I exhibit this type of behavior, it is usually reserved for unusual situations—like when one of my favorite celebrities unexpectedly dies or when Doritos stops making its Taco flavor, yet again.

I staggered into the bathroom. I splashed water onto my face. I entered a stall, fell to my knees, and feverishly thanked the good Lord above that I was not born with such a small imagination that I thought it was possible for me to see everything on the Internet. Wow!

When you get into work today, steal this whole story. In fact, steal them all—I encourage that type of activity. Just make sure you change the person in the story that saw all of the Internet to your neighbor down the street. Share it with your co-workers and feel a warm glow of kinship within your dysfunctional 8–5 family. It'll be a bonding moment.

Can't remember my story already, but want the same result? Bring in some donuts. And not just glazed ones—make sure you have some sprinkles, and some chocolate ones, and jelly, and some cake ones. Donuts are the great equalizer of any office situation

Health-crazed jogger guy may complain at first, but he will sneak one when everybody leaves the room. If you can tell the story as you are handing out donuts, you might even get a raise today.

Notice: I said "might."

14

MINT CONDITION

~

*D*o you like to barbecue? It's not just about the food, it's a way of life in Texas. Where I live, here in Austin, we have many acclaimed barbecue establishments, including the now world-famous Franklin Barbecue, which was voted Best Barbecue Joint in America by Bon Appetit. Down the road from Austin, there are four tremendous barbecue restaurants in Lockhart, Texas. I once took my parents on a "Barbecue Crawl," where we hit all four Lockhart places in a single afternoon. I had to loosen my belt for that one. Keep traveling away from Lockhart and it's almost impossible to miss City Market in Luling, Texas. I'm getting hungry just typing this story. Bottom line, always get some good brisket if you visit the Central Texas area.

Because of the fame of the restaurant, however, the line at Franklin Barbecue can last several hours. I just don't have the time or patience to do that more than once or twice a year. No worries, there are at least a dozen other barbecue places in Austin that are fantastic. We maintain a chart at work, read the annual Texas Monthly barbecue rankings, and even have the barbecue app on our phones. This story, however, is not about all of that great barbecue. It's about the game within the barbecue game—it's a about the mints.

At many of the barbecue restaurants in Texas, there is a bowl of mints (usually Starlight Mints). It's always fun to pick up a few of them to conclude the experience. It's not something you usually plan ahead of time—until now.

Lately, barbecue has become quite expensive. Some places have increased the prices of their barbecue lunch plates from $7 or $8 to as high as $13 and $15. In fact, briskets have hit $25 a pound at the highest-priced places. Suffice to say that barbecue lunches are now more of a special occasion, not an every week thing. You know the drill—make a wrong call and you could land in trouble at home for spending way too much on your work lunch.

In addition to my wife being a CPA, I work with a bunch of accountants. It's a good thing. What this means for me is that I am a part of a group of people who are always looking for the best deals or the best examples of added value.

That said, earlier in the year, I went to lunch with a couple of work friends who are accountants. We frowned when we noticed that the prices at the barbecue place we once prized for being inexpensive had gone up yet again. It was too late in our lunch hour to leave, so we tried to configure our orders so as to feel like we received some sort of added value.

I jokingly said that we were going to have to grab several extra mints at the end of the meal to help balance the rising prices. To that end, I later went by the mint bowl several times, grabbing a handful during each visit. When we returned to work, I pulled them out of my pocket and counted them. I proudly proclaimed that I owned 21 mints. I challenged my co-workers to top that total. We all laughed about it, and a couple of guys even said they had accepted my challenge.

Since the prices had gone up on all of the lunch specials at this particular barbecue joint, it was at least a couple of months before we went there to eat again. It was a birthday lunch for a co-worker. I kind of forgot that I had previously set a challenge to beat my record of 21 mints. There was not even talk of mints in the line as we placed our orders.

It was a good lunch, with lively conversation, and my friend Marc was the first to finish. He had cleaned his plate thoroughly. Still, once he finished, he went to the front of the restaurant and asked for a medium-sized to-go box. We all found this curious. From there, he walked straight to the mint bowl and began tossing mints into the box. I have never before and never since seen anyone get a to-go box for their mints. It was a bold move, one that was sure to lead to a new mint record. I couldn't help but laugh as he finished filling the box, closed the lid, and marched back to the table with a smirk on his face.

Once we were back at the office, the counting began. Yes, it was easily a new record—of 42 mints. Holy cow! Marc had elevated the mint game to an impressive new level. We have not been back to this restaurant since "42 Day," but we have so much respect for the new record that we are not even going to try to break it. That's a special level of added value that makes all of us smile.

15

THURSDAY IS NOT SUPERHERO-WORTHY

~

*I*n order to better connect with you, this next story is going to be about one of America's favorite topics—superheroes. There are a lot of superhero movies out there. About every 30 minutes, a new one hits the multiplex—usually in 5D—with the world hanging in the balance. I'm pretty sure the latest Avengers movie made a billion dollars. There are just so many superheroes now that I can't really keep up with them. Forgive me for saying this, but I had no idea there was an Ant Man.

Keeping with the superhero theme, last Thursday, we had donuts at work. This doesn't happen too often, and one of my co-workers got pretty sugared-up. She walked up to me and gleefully said, "Hey, Scott. Don't you just love Thursday? Thursday is awesome. It's like a superhero. Its arrival means our work planet is safe and the week is almost over."

It was another case of twisted logic. This thought process didn't come from an extended stay at Happy Hour; it came from her scarfing down a couple of mediocre donuts before washing them down with her over-sugared coffee. For whatever reason, her logic rubbed me the wrong way. She is not Yoda. Thursday has never been and will never be superhero-worthy for me. Fridays bring the weekend. Some Mondays are holidays. That's worthy of superhero talk. Sure, I have been to some epic Thursday night Happy Hours back in the day, but I never once equated the experience to being a superhero—not even on Halloween.

So, I said to her, "Really? You're labeling an 'almost' day as awesome. Then you are throwing in superhero status? Here's the lowdown. Thursday is Robin. Friday is freakin' Batman!" She just frowned, grabbed another donut, and walked away.

If I could redo it, I would have added that she was The Joker. Sure, she was simply trying to engage in some idle office chatter with a guy that's all about idle office chatter, but she needs to be careful about her topics. Superhero matters are never to be taken lightly. DC and Marvel would be so disappointed. We're now living in a world without Stan Lee, and we're all worse for it.

On a final note—I get all of these unwanted t-shirt offers on social media now because I have clicked on them at some point. Many of them are for superhero t-shirts. One that recently amused me read, "Always be yourself, unless you can be Batman. Then, always be Batman." I didn't order it, but it sure made me smile.

SURPRISE SHOTS

~

*A*s you read this story, how would you rate your day? The scale goes from "1"—I wish a meteor would hit the Earth and do a far better job than Calgon of taking me away—to "10"—it just keeps raining money and I'm running out of places to put it. Irrespective of your score, think about what could immediately cut it down by at least half. I suspect going to the doctor and then getting three surprise shots would do the trick, right? Here's how that played out in my house.

My sons are four years apart. Jordan, the elder one, was sick one week. I stayed home with him this particular day and the best available doctor's appointment was just after the time our younger guy, Griffin, would be picked up from school.

So, later in the day, off to the doctor I headed with both boys in the car. Like a majority of people, Griff really hates getting shots. Upon learning that he had to go to the doctor as part of Jordan's appointment, Griff made it clear that he was not getting shots. I pointed out that it was Jordan who was sick and there was no reason for him to get shots. That seemed to pacify him.

At the doctor's office, there is a "sick area" of the waiting room and a "well area." Griff played with some toys in the "well area" and hit the Purell machine on the wall about six or seven times. Jordan and I waited it out in the "sick area."

All three of us went to the exam room when the nurse said that it was time. The doctor greeted us, saw Griffin, and whispered something to the nurse. She examined Jordan and prescribed some medicine. She even gave Griff a sticker along with Jordan when the appointment seemed to be winding down. Then she said, "Griffin, I notice on your chart that you need to be protected from several different things. You want to be healthy, right."

Griffin took the bait. He agreed that he wanted to be healthy. She said she was glad to hear it because Griff needed to be better protected and they were going to help him. I knew what was coming. I looked down and hoped it was just one shot on the way. When the nurse arrived, however, it was three shots.

Griff sprang out of his chair and tried to exit the room by crawling under the examination table, but Jordan blocked his path. Griff had expected no shots. He had been assured there were no shots—now there were three shots coming his way, and it wasn't even his appointment.

It took us several minutes, but we finally convinced him that getting the shots on this day was what was best for him. He worked the McDonald's drive-through and a new video game into the deal. This kid has "future sports agent" written all over him. Despite the deal, he kept yelling, "One, two, three shots—and it's not even my appointment! That's not fair!" He was right.

Life can be challenging. If your day today was reasonably but not horrifically bad, you can console yourself with the fact that at least you didn't suddenly have to get three unexpected shots.

We now refer to the whole incident as Griff "taking three for the team." Sure, lots of folks will take one for the team, but how many people will take three for the team?

DEAD CELEBRITIES WHO MAKE FAR MORE MONEY THAN YOU AND ME

❧

*N*o matter where you live, no matter what your job, you probably go to work most days thinking you are worth more than they are paying you. The next time you get depressed about your salary, here's fuel for the fire. There are lots of dead celebrities earning oodles more than you and me. That's right, you and I are busting our butts working really hard (most days), and they still earn a lot more Benjamins than us each year, despite the fact that they are dead.

To help make us far more miserable, *Forbes* magazine was kind enough to put together a list of the top dead celebrity earners. The article is called "Money From Heaven." Before we count down the top dead celebrity earners, who do you think made the list? I correctly guessed many of them, but the person that I guessed to be Number One on the list turned out to be only Number Four.

Before we begin, here were some people that just missed making the Top 10. Elizabeth Taylor earned $8 Million this past year. Steve

McQueen earned $9 Million, and David Bowie earned $10.5 Million for the year.

Now, here is your Top 10 List.

NUMBER TEN: Bettie Page ($11 Million)

The 1950's "Queen of the Pinups" left us on December 11, 2008. She was 85 years old. Page was one of the earliest "Playmates of the Month" for Playboy magazine. Did you know that in 1959 she converted to Christianity and worked for Billy Graham? The pin-up legend had a resurgence in public interest in the 1980's and tirelessly worked to properly license her name and image. The value of her estate grows each year.

NUMBER NINE: Albert Einstein ($11.5 Million)

Albert Einstein was a German-born theoretical physicist. He developed the theory of relativity, one of the two pillars of modern physics. The other is quantum mechanics (Yes, I had to look it up). He received the 1921 Nobel Prize in Physics. Einstein published more than 300 scientific papers and more than 150 non-scientific works. His intellect rendered the word "Einstein" synonymous with "genius." Einstein passed away on April 18, 1955 at the age of 76.

NUMBER EIGHT: John Lennon ($12 Million)

English musician and peace activist John Winston Ono Lennon was a co-founder of The Beatles, the most commercially successful band in the history of popular music. Along with Paul McCartney, George Harrison, and Ringo Starr, the group ascended to worldwide fame in the 1960's. Lennon had a successful solo career after The Beatles broke up in 1970. He had married Yoko Ono a year earlier, in 1969, and had added "Ono" to his full name. Lennon had 25 number-one singles on the US Billboard Hot 100 chart as a writer, co-writer, or performer. *Rolling Stone* ranked him the fifth-greatest singer of all time. Lennon was shot and killed on December 8, 1980 in the archway of his Manhattan apartment building by Mark David Chapman. Lennon was just 40 years old.

NUMBER SEVEN: Theodor "Dr. Seuss" Geisel ($20 Million)

Theodor Seuss Geisel was a beloved American children's author, political cartoonist, and animator, best known for writing and illustrating more than 60 books under the pen name Dr. Seuss. By the time of his death, he'd sold more than 600 million copies of his books and been translated into more than 20 languages. He adopted the name "Dr. Seuss" while he was an undergraduate at Dartmouth. Geisel's birthday, March 2, has been adopted as the annual date for National Read Across America Day. His work has spawned 11 television specials, five feature films, a Broadway musical, and four television series. He died of oral cancer on September 24, 1991 at the age of 87. His many honors include two Academy Awards, two Emmy Awards, a Peabody Award, and the Pulitzer Prize. In 2000, *Publisher's Weekly* compiled a list of the 100 best-selling children's books of all-time. Dr. Seuss wrote 16 of them, with the best-selling being *Green Eggs and Ham*, ranked #4. Author's Note: One of my favorite books of all time is *Oh, the Places You'll Go!* by Dr. Seuss.

NUMBER SIX: Bob Marley ($21 Million)

The Jamaican singer-songwriter has been gone since 1981. He died of Melanoma at the young age of 36. Ironically, his final words were reported to have been "Money can't buy life." Even today, however, people want to buy Marley products. Marley is credited with popularizing reggae music around the world. Marley's music gains new fans each year. He's considered the face of Jamaica by many. The merchandising of Marley products continues to grow, and the revenue opportunities seem limitless.

NUMBER FIVE: Prince ($25 Million)

Prince Rogers Nelson was an American singer, songwriter, musician, record producer, and filmmaker. Born and raised in Minneapolis, Minnesota, Prince wrote his first song at the age of seven. He was known for having a wide vocal range, a flamboyant stage presence, a fashion sensibility, a love for the color purple, and a flair for eclectic work. His album *Purple Rain* spent 24 weeks atop the *Billboard 200* albums chart. His music blended the genres of funk, dance, and rock. Prince has sold more than 100 million records worldwide and is one of the best-selling music artists of all time. He won eight Grammy Awards, six American Music Awards, a Golden Globe Award, and an Academy Award. Prince passed away at the age of 57 on April 21, 2016.

NUMBER FOUR: Elvis Presley ($27 Million)

This is one of several people that I correctly guessed was on the list, but I incorrectly guessed that Elvis was Number One. Often referred to as the "King of Rock and Roll," Presley is one of the most celebrated and influential musicians of all-time. He is the best-selling solo artist in the history of recorded music. In fact, he received the Grammy Lifetime Achievement Award at age 36. His music has been commercially successful in many genres, including pop, country, blues, and gospel. We lost The King on August 16, 1977, to a heart attack. He was just 42. Of course, some people still believe that he faked his death and is living somewhere in obscurity. I like the idea of that, but I personally don't think that's what happened. Elvis earned $35 million this past year. Even though that's a lot of dough, I expected the number to be even higher.

NUMBER THREE: ARNOLD PALMER ($40 Million)

Professional golfer Arnold Palmer lived to be 87 years old. He died on September 25, 2016. The famous golfer is considered one of the greatest and most charismatic players in the history of the sport. He was the first superstar of the sport's television age. His career spanned more than six decades. He won 62 PGA Tour titles and was one of the 13 original inductees into the World Gold Hall of Fame. His business acumen was just as sharp as his golf game. He designed more than 300 golf courses in more than 25 countries on five continents. You may enjoy drinking his branded beverage, the Arnold Palmer; it combines sweet iced tea with lemonade.

NUMBER TWO: Charles Schultz ($48 Million)

Checking in at the Number Two spot is Peanuts creator Charles Schulz. Charles died in his sleep on February 12, 2000 at the age of 77. He had colon cancer. Just before his death, Schultz had decided to retire after doing the Peanuts strip for 50 years. The last original Peanuts strip was published the day after his death on Sunday, February 13, 2000. Schultz had predicted that the strip would outlive him, since the strips were usually drawn weeks before their publication. A really cool thing happened on May 27, 2000 when cartoonists of more than 100 strips paid homage to him by incorporating his Peanuts characters into their strips. Classic Peanuts comic strips continue to run in newspapers, and Peanuts TV shows, movies, and merchandise remain popular even today. It's hard to imagine a world without Charlie Brown and friends. It still makes me mad when I think about how many times Lucy pulled the football away from my boy Chuck.

DRUM ROLL, PLEASE

NUMBER ONE: MICHAEL JACKSON ($825 MILLION)

Michael Joseph Jackson died on June 25, 2009, of a cardiac arrest. He was 50 years old then. The King of Pop was one of the most popular entertainers of all-time. He was a global celebrity for more than four decades. *Thriller* remains the best-selling album of all time. The Guinness Book has declared him the Most Successful Entertainer of All Time. He won 13 Grammy Awards and 24 American Music

Awards. It is estimated that he has sold more than 350 million records worldwide. According to Forbes, he has been the top-earning dead celebrity each year since his death.

The next time you are doing something you don't want to do at work, just think—Michael Jackson will be earning more than $2 million that day, and he is not even with us anymore.

GROCERY STORE MATH

∽

I often like swinging by the grocery store after work and grabbing exactly 15 items. It's 15 items because that is supposed to be the limit on the number of items you can have in the express checkout lane. It's also a perfect amount of items to place in one of those red, handheld, carry-along baskets. This keeps you from needing the big metal grocery cart with the wheels that often roll in several different directions or lock up at inopportune moments. I love driving the big cart and filling it (sometimes with basketball shots) on a big store run, but not on a 15-item run.

While I'm stopping short of calling it grocery store terrorism, I want to report something you probably already know. New math has gained a foothold in our grocery stores. It's math we never learned in any classroom. It is not the metric system. It is not a Sting song.

What I'm trying to say is it seems that 15 items can now mean as many as 24 items. That's how many items the guy in front of me had the other day—24. And, he seemed pretty proud of it. He was the happiest guy in the store. He had no worries about being over the 15-item limit.

This is just the latest chapter in what is now a never-ending book of over-the-item limit stories that are unfolding while I stand in line. Earlier that same week in the same grocery store line, a tough guy in a half-buttoned sleeveless shirt had 22 items. He looked around with a glare just daring anybody to call him out on it.

And it's not just a guy thing. Last month, this very pleasant older lady announced to me that she was sorry that she had 17 items but her grandkids were coming over. This meant she needed some extra things, but the big cart was too heavy for her to push. What could I do but look at her, smile, and say, "It's all good." I could stomach her 17 items, but the whole process is out of whack.

I know there are real problems out there. People are homeless. Countries are fighting wars. Nobody seems to agree on politics. But interwoven into this dynamic is the fact that most all of us have to go to the grocery store.

I used to feel bad if I even thought about sneaking in a 16th item during the checkout process. Now, I think I'm one of the few people who really has 15 items. Is everybody else laughing at me because I'm playing by the rules? I feel like I have a neon "chump" sign flashing over my head that everybody in the grocery store can see except me. Does that lady even have grandkids? Do they chuckle all the way to their cars thinking about what a sucker I am for not having more than 15 items?

Where does all this madness stop? I'm betting that before I can even get this story published, somebody will break the current record of 24 items. As of now, I've never seen a store clerk call anybody out for being over the limit. Does this ever happen?

Never fear, Fun Stories Nation. I've recently gone to my happy place to deal with this grocery store madness. I have convinced myself that I am doing research for a hidden-camera show. The show awards points to shoppers for every item they successfully check out past the 15-item limit. How many items can they get before a store clerk calls them out for being over the limit?

Good game shows need a twist. Sometimes, in my pretend grocery game show, there is a "Good Citizen Award." This happens when a person is rewarded for having exactly 15 items and not going over. I'm thinking a fun prize would be to give them 15 seconds of free shopping. That would bring positive attention to those who play by the rules.

I don't have a name for the show yet. If you have a clever name idea, please send it to us on the Facebook page or tweet it to us @mentalkickball. You can also torture me with pictures of how many items you've successfully gotten away with checking out in the 15-item line.

If you're keeping score at home, this grocery item limit is morphing into its own currency exchange rate. Right now, 15 = 24 is the way I would try to define that exchange rate.

Happy shopping!

NEXT LEVEL BUREAUCRACY

~

CW e could hold a day-long discussion about the many quirky things that happened at the various jobs you have worked. Here is one that I remembered the other day when one of the news channels discussed government bureaucracy.

I once worked at a place that I will call Company A. At Company A, it became fashionable to handle key issues by forming task forces. At first, it seemed like a very efficient way to handle things. Sales went up, problems seemed to diminish, and everything seemed great.

As we've learned from superhero movies, however, with great power (and success) comes great responsibility. As Company A basked in its success, it decided that almost every issue in the building was worthy of its own separate task force. Lively discussions of key issues turned into a multi-page spreadsheet of task-force topics. We were constantly voting by e-mail on possible new task forces.

Before too long, I was personally on eight task forces for Company A. There were now more task force meetings than a person's normal work day could handle. This meant that most of us were working till later and later each night. Work morale began to decline. Production began to decline. The era of quick-fix solutions was ending for Company A.

I turned down three more task force requests and started assigning some of my employees to the newest task forces. The inevitable soon happened.

Company A had to form a task force to track all of its task forces.

That moment seemed to have walked right out of a *Dilbert* comic strip. There were highlighters and Excel spreadsheets everywhere. So, I begged my way out of serving on the Task Force Tracker or "TFT" and sent a heartfelt e-mail that closed with the line, "May the task forces be with you."

That was a few jobs ago. I'm not sure how many task forces Company A has in place today. Yes, I gained some valuable experience in some key areas by being on the task forces and I am grateful for the opportunities that were afforded to me by Company A. I often wonder, however, how many task forces does it take to tip the scale and turn bureaucracy into "bureaucrazy." Maybe we can all form a task force to figure it out!

FUN QUIZ FROM THE TWITTERVERSE

~

*E*ven if you don't enjoy Twitter, it's still fun to take a look at some of the most followed people on the popular social media site. Because we just love pitting things against one another, we're going to give you some celebrity Twitter matchups. You can guess which celebrity has more Twitter followers and then we'll give you the right answer. At the end of the story, we'll tell you which celebrity has the most Twitter followers as of the time of writing of this book.

If you are reading this book many years into the future, you can laugh heartily that we once followed these people. Does Twitter even exist anymore, future people? Think of this as a Twitter time capsule if you're in that situation. With a big tip of the cap to countdown gurus Casey Kasem and Ryan Seacrest, here we go, Fun Stories Nation.

BATTLE NUMBER ONE
  LeBron James vs. Oprah Winfrey

(BOXING BELL SOUND EFFECT)

Which celebrity has more Twitter followers?
Make your final answer.…
And the winner is…

Oprah Winfrey. As of writing this, both have more than 41 million followers, but Oprah has about 60,000 more than King James. At the time of writing this, Oprah ranked 26th for most Twitter followers and LeBron ranked 27th.

BATTLE NUMBER TWO
    Justin Bieber vs. Justin Timberlake
    (BOXING BELL SOUND EFFECT)

Which celebrity has more Twitter followers?
    Make your final answer…
    And the winner is…

Justin Bieber. JT has more than 64 million Twitter followers. That makes him the 10th most popular person on Twitter. The Biebs, however, has more than 104 million Twitter followers. That's a lot of folks, which makes him the 2nd most followed person on Twitter.

BATTLE NUMBER THREE
    Donald Trump vs. Bruno Mars
    (BOXING BELL SOUND EFFECT)

Which celebrity has more Twitter followers?

Make your final answer...
And the winner is...

Donald Trump. Sure, it definitely helps if you're the President and you do much of your communication through tweets. President Trump has more than 55 million Twitter followers, making him the 16th most followed person on Twitter. Bruno Mars has more than 42 million Twitter followers, putting him behind as the 25th most followed person on Twitter.

BATTLE NUMBER FOUR
Rihanna vs. Taylor Swift
(BOXING BELL SOUND EFFECT)

Which celebrity has more Twitter followers?
Make your final answer...
And the winner is...

Rihanna. Rihanna has more than 88 million Twitter followers, which makes her the 4th most followed person on Twitter. Right behind Rihanna, T-Swizzle comes in as the 5th most followed person on Twitter with more than 83 million followers.

FINAL BATTLE
Drake vs. Lady Gaga
(BOXING BELL SOUND EFFECT)

Which celebrity has more Twitter followers?
Make your final answer...
And the winner is...

. . .

Lady Gaga. Gaga has more than 77 million Twitter followers and ranks as the 6th most popular person on Twitter, while Drake ranks 33rd. Drizzy has more than 37 million Twitter followers.

MOST POPULAR PERSON ON TWITTER
Who's perched at the pinnacle of the Twitterverse?
(TIMPANI SOUND EFFECT)

It's singer Katy Perry (as if I had to put the word "singer" in front of her name). She has more than 106 million Twitter followers. She's simply @katyperry on Twitter if you would like to help add to her lead.

Three more people of note who were not mentioned during this battle are Barack Obama (103 million followers, 3rd most popular), Ellen DeGeneres (76 million followers, 7th most popular), and Cristiano Ronaldo (75 million followers, 8th most popular).

Well, that's it. We've reached the end of the book. Thank you for reading FS4. If, for whatever reason, this is your first *Fun Stories* experience, I'd like to alert you to watch for bonus material that often appears after the end of the regular chapters. Did it happen this time? Keep turning the pages to find out!

As Casey Kasem used to say, keep your feet on the ground and keep reaching for the stars!

R. SCOTT MURPHY'S AMAZON AUTHOR SITE

R. SCOTT MURPHY ON APPLE MUSIC AND ITUNES

AFTERWORD

POST-GAME SHOW

Thank you for reading this book! If you enjoyed it, please consider giving it an honest Amazon review. I'm an indie author and your voice counts. Now, if you keep turning the pages, you might just find some for fun!

YOU'RE IN THE BONUS ROUND!

BONUS MATERIAL

Here you are again, sniffing out the bonus material. Nice job! I like to call this the "Ferris Bueller Time." It's the bonus information after the credits roll. For me, it's an integral part of the *Fun Stories* formula.

This time around, I want to share some additional information related to the frozen dinners mentioned earlier in this book. I also want to share some bonus information for the Old MacDonald story, including a fun list of animal noises that can be incorporated into a fun game. You can play the game with kids or you can turn it into a drinking game for adults.

BONUS MATERIAL

BONUS STORY

FROZEN DINNER WINNERS

What started out as a slight grocery store annoyance in the NASA story in this book led to a full-on Internet expedition about frozen dinners. I must confess that it was beyond interesting. Wow, some people can't post enough on the Internet about frozen dinners. I get it when you post way too many pictures of your kids, or your pet, or your new house, or someone you're dating who is way out of your league. But this one person had more than 100 pictures of the different frozen dinners that he had eaten in life. Dude needs one of three things: a girlfriend, a boyfriend, or a blow-up doll. Upon further review, Mr. 100+ Frozen Dinner Post Guy might just need all three—and possibly at the same time.

It had me sitting there just randomly saying, "Hungry-Man," over and over. I'm also guessing Mr. 100+ Frozen Dinner Post Guy doesn't enjoy sports. I would, however, love to hear a hip-hop song where the chorus goes, "Hungry-Man, Hungry-Man," over and over. Maybe Macklemore & Ryan Lewis could record it as a companion volume to "Thrift Shop." (SCOTT SINGS) *I'm gonna get some gravy...*

Another group of folks had a discussion thread about frozen dinners that has been going on for more than four years. That's a longer amount of time than some Presidential administrations. These folks regularly post about how the flavor has changed on some of the frozen meals, how the portions are slightly smaller now, and how the price keeps getting higher. Of all of the topics in the world, this is what they chose to talk about? That's definitely my type of random!

There's a fun article on thrillist.com where they taste-tested nine microwave dinners. That's fun stuff that you should consider reading. The reader comments about the taste of microwave meals ranged from the highly positive, "Delight on a plate," to the beyond negative, "Tastes like chewable secondhand cigarette smoke." There was also a hotly-contested discussion about whether pot pies, mini frozen pizzas, and frozen lasagna count as frozen dinners. There's also a microwave vs. oven frozen meal debate raging in several chat rooms.

During my continued frozen dinner binge surf, "Consumer Reports" had a whole Frozen Meals Ratings section that I thought would offer great material to write about. But when I clicked, it said "Over 6 million people subscribe to 'Consumer Reports.'" Sadly, I am not one of them, so their ratings remain a mystery.

Never fear, after an obligatory Phelps Flap (you know about this if you've read my story "I'm the Freakin' Michael Phelps of Googling"), I found Statista's ranking of the Top 10 Selling Single-Serve Frozen Dinner Brands in the United States. Casey Kasem would be so proud. Statista ranked them by sales in million US dollars. Here we go...

NUMBER 10

With 108.4 million dollars in sales, it's Weight Watchers Smart Ones. That's a smart choice!

NUMBER NINE

With 111.8 million dollars in sales, it's Michelinas. Have you tried them?

NUMBER EIGHT

With 112.9 million dollars in sales, it's Healthy Choice Top Chef Café Steamers. They also won the award for longest name in the countdown!

NUMBER SEVEN

With 126.5 million dollars in sales, you know it, some of you love it, some of you grew up with it—I know I did—it's Hungry-Man! Macklemore, please let me chime in a couple of "Hungry-Man" chants when you record that song!

NUMBER SIX

With 128 million in sales, it's Lean Cuisine Simple Favorites. See, frozen dinners don't have to be complicated—just find some simple favorites.

NUMBER FIVE

With 136.3 million in sales, it's Healthy Choice Café Steamers. Even without the presence of a Top Chef, it's still so steamy!

NUMBER FOUR

With a hearty 232.8 million in sales, it's Banquet. Sidebar, I wonder if

Banquet and Coors, "the banquet beer," have ever considered a collaboration. Call me!

NUMBER THREE

We're getting really far into the countdown now. These dinners made a whopping 246.9 million dollars from sales. Ladies and gentlemen, it's the Lean Cuisine Culinary Collection.

NUMBER TWO

Having sold 398.6 million dollars of frozen dinners, it's Marie Callendar's.

NUMBER ONE

The Number One single-serve frozen dinner brand—with 518.7 million in sales... Stouffer's. Congratulations! I'm betting Stouffer's also gets the most "delight on a plate" reviews.

If you didn't like where your favorite finished, get more of them the next time you're at the grocery store. I have to offer an official apology to that Kenny Rogers shirt wearin', check book forgettin' 80s lady—frozen dinners are back on my radar.

(SCOTT SINGS—BADLY)
I'm gonna get some gravy...

MORE BONUS MATERIAL

BONUS INFORMATION AND GAME

THE LEAST AMOUNT OF FAME POSSIBLE
(OLD MACDONALD RIDES AGAIN)

Following my revelation to you that I've spent some time in the character of Old MacDonald, I've been surfing for even more information
about Old Mac. In fact, I found a fun list of animal sounds on Wikipedia that you can use the next time you sing the Old MacDonald
song with your kids. Alternate idea, why do kids get all of the fun?
You can turn this list into a fun drinking game with a bunch of your
co-workers at your next happy hour.

Based on my limited fame as Old MacDonald, I recommend the list. It
contains 75 animals. I found the "List of animal sounds" because it
linked from the Old MacDonald entry on Wikipedia. Next to each
animal, I've listed the sound it makes, and then assigned it a point
value. You get more points for the more difficult animals.

For example, pigs, cows, and cats have sounds that are easily identifiable. Hence, they're worth less points. Apparently, the Old MacDonald that Wikipedia featured for its "List of animal sounds" had a huge farm. I never expected Old Mac to have lions, elephants, hippos, giraffes, walruses, and whales on the farm, but it makes the game more fun.

Honestly, once you've had a few drinks (soda, juice boxes, or liquor drinks), I think I would allow any reasonable animal noise to be used in the game. Give five points for more unique animals all the way down to one point for an easy animal sound. I define an easy animal sound as one that a five-year-old can quickly identify. If you've turned this into a drinking game (liquor) and you don't have any five-year-olds in the room—choose the person that is most acting like a five-year-old to be the official scorer.

If you don't like the point values, you can change them to whatever you like. This is a very flexible game. The person who earns the most points wins—well, really, everybody wins when you play this fun game. Enjoy!

- Antelope (snort—4 points)
- Badgers (growl—4 points)
- Bats (screech—3 points)
- Bears (growl—2 points)
- Bees (buzz—1 point)
- Birds (chirp—1 point)
- Bitterns (boom—5 points)
- Cats (meow—1 point)
- Chickens (cluck, cock-a-doodle-doo—1 point)
- Chimpanzees (scream—2 points)
- Chinchillas (squeak—4 points)
- Cicadas (chirp—3 points)
- Cows (moo—1 point)
- Crickets (chirp—2 points)

- Crows (caw, cah—2 points)
- Curlews (pipe—5 points)
- Deer (bellow, bleat—3 points)
- Dogs (bark—1 point)
- Dolphins (click—2 points)
- Donkeys (hee-haw—2 points)
- Ducks (quack—1 point)
- Eagles (screech—4 points)
- Elephants (trumpet—2 points)
- Elk (bugle—4 points)
- Ferrets (dook—3 points)
- Frogs (croak—1 point)
- Giraffes (bleat—4 points)
- Geese (honk—2 points)
- Goats (bleet—3 points)
- Grasshoppers (chirp—2 points)
- Guinea Pigs (squeak—3 points)
- Hamsters (squeak—3 points)
- Hermit Crabs (chirp—3 points)
- Hippos (growl—3 points)
- Hogs (grunt, squeal—2 points)
- Horses (neigh, whinny—2 points)
- Hyenas (laugh—3 points)
- Jaguars (growl—3 points)
- Lambs (bleat—2 points)
- Leopards (growl—3 points)
- Linnets (chuckle—5 points)
- Lions (growl—2 points)
- Magpies (chatter—5 points)
- Mice (squeak—3 points)
- Monkeys (scream—1 point)
- Moose (bellow—3 points)
- Mosquitos (buzz—2 points)
- Okapis (cough, bellow—5 points)
- Oxen (moo—3 points)

- Owls (hoot—2 points)
- Parrots (talking, squawk—2 points)
- Peacocks (scream—4 points)
- Pigeons (coo—2 points)
- Pigs (oink—1 point)
- Prairie Dogs (bark—2 points)
- Rabbits (squeak—2 points)
- Raccoons (trill—2 points)
- Rats (squeak—3 points)
- Ravens (caw—3 points)
- Rhinos (bellow—5 points)
- Rooks (caw—5 points)
- Seals (bark—2 points)
- Sheep (baa—1 point)
- Snakes (hiss—1 point)
- Swans (cry, hiss—3 points)
- Tapirs (squeak—5 points)
- Tarantulas (hiss—3 points)
- Tigers (growl—2 points)
- Toads (croak—2 points)
- Tokay Geckos (croak—4 points)
- Turkeys (gobble—1 point)
- Vultures (scream—2 points)
- Walruses (groan—3 points)
- Whales (sing—4 points)
- Wolves (howl—2 points)

REVIEWERS NEEDED

YOUR VOICE COUNTS

I know I'm repeating myself, but this is really important to independent authors like me. If you enjoyed this book, please consider giving it an honest Amazon review. Reviews make a huge difference. You're a difference maker, right? Thank you for your consideration.

R. Scott Murphy's Amazon Author Site

ABOUT THE AUTHOR

R. Scott Murphy looks at the world in fun, sometimes twisted, ways. He is the madcap mind behind the *Fun Stories* series of humorous eBooks, albums, and audiobooks. Part storyteller, part game-show host, part DJ, and part madcap tour guide, the award-winning author resides in Austin, Texas, with his wife, two sons, and a rescue dog named "Curly."

Murphy holds a master's degree from the University of Missouri School of Journalism and has taught advertising at the University of Texas. An experienced TV and radio personality, stadium announcer, advertising writer, TV game-show producer, and sports producer, he uses his many experiences as inspiration for *Fun Stories*.

Murphy is a four-time winner of the "Late Show with David Letterman" Top 10 List Contest, plus a Remi Award winner for script writing. The first three eBooks in the *Fun Stories* series reached #1 on Amazon Humor. Numerous audio versions of Murphy's stories have charted on the iTunes Comedy Songs rankings. "Chick-fil-A Makes Me Feel Like Leonardo DiCaprio," "I'm the Freakin' Michael Phelps of

Googling," and "Shamelessly Suggestive City Names" all hit #1. Check out Apple Music, Amazon, and Spotify for Murphy's complete audio catalogue.

Murphy enjoys playing loud music, learning air guitar, watching sports, reviewing all the oddball shows he records on his DVRs, and collecting vinyl and CD versions of the classic *American Top 40* radio show with Casey Kasem.

BOOKS BY R. SCOTT MURPHY

Fun Stories For Your Drive To Work

Fun Stories For Your Drive Home

Fun Stories: Random City Limits

Fun Stories: Searching For More Cowbell

Fun Stories Greatest Hits

Fun Stories Box Set (Books 1-5)

Ducks on the Pond

AUDIOBOOKS BY R. SCOTT MURPHY

Fun Stories For Your Drive To Work

Fun Stories For Your Drive Home

Fun Stories: Random City Limits

ALBUMS BY R. SCOTT MURPHY

Fun Stories For Your Drive To Work

Fun Stories For Your Drive Home

Fun Stories: Random City Limits

iTUNES COMEDY SINGLES BY R. SCOTT MURPHY

Chick-fil-A Makes Me Feel Like Leonardo DiCaprio

I'm the Freakin' Michael Phelps of Googling

Shamefully Suggestive City Names

Happy Friday (Mr. Pee Man)

Cub Scout Dropout

George Clooney Time

Good Folks, Bad Coaching (Four-Year-Old Soccer)

Chick-fil-A: The Rest of the Leonardo DiCaprio Story

THANK YOU FOR READING AND LISTENING!

ACKNOWLEDGMENTS

PHOTO CREDITS

Thank you to all of the good folks who were kind enough to offer free images on Pixabay for use by indie artists such as myself. Please review their creative work on Pixabay and consider hiring them for your next project.

Searching For More Cowbell (Clker-Free-Vector-Images)

The Least Amount of Fame Possible (Clker-Free-Vector-Images)

Not the Next Carrie Underwood (josemairing)

Ridiculous Movie Theater Recipes: Bigfoot Popcorn (OpenClipart-Vectors)

How NASA Thins The Herd (wikiimages)

Fraudulent Texas Messages (Falkenpost)

Bonus Material (Vivs4e)

Frozen Dinner Winners (elasticcomputefarm)

The Least Amount of Fame Possible (Clker-Free-Vector-Images)

Your Voice Counts (TKaucic)

Get More Fun (Tumisu)

FUN STORIES NATION WANTS YOU

GET MORE FUN AND FREE STUFF

Keep the fun going! Get fun updates, free stuff, and more info about Scott's latest projects. Join Fun Stories Nation by subscribing at www.mentalkickball.com.

Made in the USA
Coppell, TX
28 July 2020